GRADE
5

Success With **Writing**

New York • Toronto • London • Auckland • Sydney
Mexico City • New Delhi • Hong Kong • Buenos Aires

Teaching *Resources*

State Standards Correlations

To find out how this book helps you meet your state's standards, log on to **www.scholastic.com/ssw**

Written by Barbara Adams
Cover design by Ka-Yeon Kim-Li
Interior illustrations by Susan Hendron
Interior design by Quack & Company

ISBN 978-0-545-20075-2

23 24   40   20 19

Introduction

One of the greatest challenges teachers face is helping students develop independent writing skills. Each writing experience is unique and individualized, making it each student's responsibility to plan, expand, and proofread his or her work. However, the high-interest topics and engaging exercises in this book will both stimulate and encourage young students as they develop the necessary skills to become independent writers. This book uses these strategies to introduce grade-appropriate skills that can be used in daily writing assignments such as journals, stories, and letters. Like a stepladder, this book will help students reach the next level of independent writing.

Table of Contents

Body Facts

A **sentence** is a group of words that expresses a complete thought. There are four kinds of sentences.

A **declarative sentence** is a **statement**. It gives information and ends with a period.
   I just finished a really cool article about the body.

An **interrogative sentence** is a **question**. It asks for information and often begins with who, what, where, when, why, *or* how. *A question ends with a question mark.*
   What is the title of the article?

An **imperative sentence** is a **command**. It tells or asks someone to do something. A command usually ends with a period but can also end with an exclamation point.
   Tell me where you read it. Hurry up and tell me!

An **exclamatory sentence** is an **exclamation**.
It shows strong feeling or emotion and ends with an exclamation point.
   I can't wait to read it now!

Use any or all of the words in each group to write four kinds of sentences. One sentence has been completed for you. Begin and end each sentence correctly.

do how you many times breathe minute is per that count twenty humans fast

Interrogative: How many times per minute do humans breathe?

Declarative: Humans breathe fast when they panic.

Imperative: You will count how meny times you breathe in twenty minutes.

Exclamatory: I can not belive that humans can run so fast in under twenty minutes!

sixty-five believe the is body water about percent I it don't really

Interrogative: About How water do we really need in our body every day?

Declarative: The human body is about 65/sixty five percent water.

Imperative: I don't really believe this therory is accyoret.

Exclamatory: I dont believe my body is water!

how did read small twenty-two long you are the feet about intestines

Interrogative: How did the intestines of twenty-two long feet come?

Declarative: The small body of a human intestines 22 inches tall.

Imperative: You are twenty two, how do you still read a small 22 page book about feet.

Exclamatory: Your feet are small and long chaheha!

Get the Scoop

Have you ever interviewed anyone? What kinds of questions did you ask? Were they clear and complete? Who, What, Where, When, Why, or How at the beginning of a sentence usually signals a question. A helping verb such as Is, Are, Was, Were, Do, Does, Did, Can, or Could at the beginning of a sentence also signals a question.

How did you get your start?

Did you get your start in school?

What was your first role?

Was Peter Pan your first role?

Why do you enjoy acting?

Do you enjoy acting because it's fun?

Which kinds of questions do you think would help you gather more information?

For each category, write the name of a person you would like to interview. Then write several questions you would ask to learn more about the person. Try to avoid questions with *yes* or *no* answers.

1. **an interesting fictional character:** _Connor and Alex Baliy_

_____

_____

2. **an early explorer:** _____

_____

_____

3. **a favorite rock star:** _____

_____

_____

4. **someone you admire:** _____

_____

_____

5. **an elderly person:** _____

_____

_____

6. **a founding father of the United States:** _____

_____

Think of a person in your everyday life you could interview, such as a grandparent, business owner, local politician, or police officer. Ask to interview the person. Prepare a list of questions ahead of time. Record the person's responses. Share the results with friends, classmates, or family members.

Clearly Interesting

 A sentence may be very simple, but you can make it more interesting by adding adverbs, adjectives, and prepositional phrases. When you add to a sentence, you expand it.

The kitten ran.

adjectives   adverb   prepositional phrase

The frightened, little kitten ran quickly under the bed.

Add to each list of adjectives, adverbs, and prepositional phrases that has been started.

Adjectives	**Adverbs**	**Prepositional Phrases**	
lonely	calmly	over the bridge	with my friends
old	eagerly	through the woods	until noon
friendly	continuously	across the lake	of commuters
beautiful	frequently	out of the building	toward the moon
cranky	yesterday	during rush hour	into the water

Small	angerly	Under the Bed to find my toy
mad	madly	Over the heystack of hey
happy	happly	Past the farmer to get the rade
young	wonderfully	around the puddle while playing tag
tall	asomorlly	baside the Barn in the water

Use some of the words and phrases from above to expand each sentence.

1. **The baby cried.** The cranky baby cryed continuosly during
   night time.

2. **Thousands left.** Thousands of people left lonely and angerly during
   rush hour.

3. **The man walked.** The old man walked haply out of the
   bilding.

4. **The students sat.** The small young students sat camly over
   the carpet.

5. **I went.** I Joged quietly and caltmly AS I went under the bridge.
   _____

 A complete sentence has two parts. The subject part tells whom or what the sentence is about. The predicate part tells what the subject is or does. Reread the sentences you expanded. Draw a line between the subject part and the predicate part.

Sentence Sense

➡️ *It is important to choose and arrange the words and phrases in your sentences so that what you intend to say is clear to your readers.*

Eating a bowl of curds and whey, a spider frightened Miss Muffet away.

Who was eating the curds and whey, the spider or Miss Muffet? You are probably familiar with the nursery rhyme, so you know that it was Miss Muffet, but the intended meaning is not clear in the above sentence. Notice the difference in the revised sentence.

While Miss Muffet was eating a bowl of curds and whey, a spider frightened her away.

The intended meaning is unclear in the sentences below. Rearrange each sentence to make the meaning clear. As you revise, remember that you can also add and remove words. There may be more than one possible way to fix each sentence.

1. **When she was just a puppy, my sister taught Sunshine many tricks.**
When Sunshine was just a puppy, My sister taught many tricks to Sunshine.

2. **The students cheered for their team in the bleachers.**
The students cheered for their team in the bleachers.

3. **My mother for teasing my little brother scolded me.**
My mother scolded at me, for teasing my little brother.

4. **The saleswoman sold shirts to the tourists with rainbows on them.**
The saleswoman sold shirts with rainbows on them to the touris[t]

5. **As a preschooler, Dad taught me to read.**
My Dad taught me to read, because I am a preschooler.

6. **Perching on top of the cage, I noticed that our parakeet was missing a tail feather.**
I noticed that our tailfeather was missing on our parake[et]

7. **Wading in the shallow water, just 20 feet away porpoises were swimming from us.**
Porpoise twenty feet away, Wading in the shallow water.

8. **Grandma has a garden behind the old, dilapidated shed that is unbelievable.**
Unbelievable! Grandma has a garden behind the old shed.

9. **While emptying the dishwasher this morning, the dog started barking at me.**
While I was emptying the dishwasher, the dog started barking at me

10. **We heard about the missing painting that was found on the news today.**
On the news today, We heard that the missing painting was found

Reread some of your recent writing. Look for several sentences in which the intended meaning is not as clear as it could be. Write the sentences on a sheet of paper. Then revise each one. Ask someone you know to read and compare each pair of sentences.

Get to the Point

When you write, it is important to be clear and concise. Sometimes a sentence can
have too many words or words that are not necessary. Compare the two sentences.

**The audience couldn't hear what the speaker was saying on account of the fact
that the microphone wasn't turned on because someone forgot.**

The audience couldn't hear the speaker because the microphone wasn't turned on.

Decide which words and phrases are not really necessary in each
sentence below and cross them out. You can also replace words or
change their position to make each sentence more clear and concise.
Write the revised sentence.

1. In your ~~own~~ opinion, do you think students should ~~have to~~ wear uniforms?

   In your opinon, do you think students should wear uniforms?

2. ~~What is incredible about the cheetah is~~ the cheetah's quickness!

   The Cheetah's are quick.

3. I drew an ~~egg-shaped~~ oval, ~~a round~~ circle, and ~~a four-sided~~ square.

   I drew an Oval, a Circle, and a square.

4. The neighborhood families worked ~~as a team all~~ together.

   The neighborhood families worked together.

5. That elephant is ~~an~~ enormous ~~elephant in~~ size!

   That elephan is enormous size!

6. The ostrich, the world's largest ~~flightless~~ bird, ~~is a big bird that can~~ run as fast as 40 miles
   per hour.

   The ostrich, the world's largest bird, they can run as fast as 40 miles per hour.

7. More than anything ~~else in the~~ whole wide world, I would ~~really like to~~ be a professional
   basketball player ~~some day in the future~~.

   More than anything else in the word I want to be a profesional Basketball player.

8. We nicknamed my brother "Carrot Top" because his hair is ~~the color~~ orange like ~~the
   color of~~ carrots.

   We nicknamed my brother Carrot Top because his hair is orange like carrot.

9. It seems to me that the best thing ~~that~~ anyone can do is ~~to always tell~~ the truth ~~no
   matter what the situation may be~~.

   It seems to me that the best thing that anyone can do is tell the truth.

💡 **There is more than one way to revise many of the sentences in the above exercise. Choose two
sentences and revise them as many different ways as you can on a sheet of paper. Then read all your
revisions. Think about which one seems the most effective and why.**

Lots of Words

Do you sometimes run together several ideas into one long, run-on sentence?

According to my grandma, it is a good idea to eat chicken soup when you have a cold and believe it or not, scientists agree with her the soup fights the stuffiness by thinning out the lining of your sinuses I think chicken soup tastes better than medicine, so the next time I have a cold I'm going to follow my grandmother's advice.

You can easily fix a run-on sentence by rewriting each complete idea as a separate sentence. Begin each sentence with a capital letter and end it with the correct punctuation mark.

According to my grandma, it is a good idea to eat chicken soup when you have a cold. Believe it or not, scientists agree with her! The soup fights the stuffiness by thinning out the lining of your sinuses. I think chicken soup tastes better than medicine, so the next time I have a cold I'm going to follow my grandmother's advice.

Rewrite each run-on sentence correctly.

1. **Did you know that carrots really are good for your eyes there is a vitamin in this crunchy orange root called beta-carotene that may help lower the risk of eye disease and so the next time you find carrot sticks in your lunch don't trade them or toss them away munch away in good health instead?**

    Did you know that Carrots reall are good for your eyes. Ther is Vitamin
    , crunchy orange root. called beta-carotende,

2. **Do you like potato chips, cookies, cake, and ice cream if you're like me, you probably do and I'm sure you also know that these wonderful taste treats are considered to be junk food and it is a good idea to eat small amounts of food with a lot of fat, oil, sugar, and salt?**

    Do you like potato, chips, cookies, cake, and Icecream
    you probly do. They are considred to be Junk food.

3. **Think about all the foods you eat and are they nutritious and do they have all the vitamins and minerals your body needs to be healthy, or are they full of fats, sugar, and salt use that information to make healthful choices because you are what you eat.**

    Think about all the food you eat. They eather have vit aning
    minerals, for you to be healthy, or full of sugar
    and fat.

Reread a report, composition, or story you have recently written. Look for run-on sentences. Then rewrite them correctly.

11-29-19

A Capital Adventure

You know that the first word of a sentence is always capitalized. Here are other rules to remember when you write.

Capitalize

- *the names of people and pets.*
  My friend, Maggie Ames, has two cats, Hero and Spike.
- *titles of respect such as Dr., Mrs., Mr., Miss, and Ms.*
  Mr. Ames and Maggie took the cats to Dr. Jones, the vet, last week.
- *the names of days, months, and holidays, but not the seasons.*
  Maggie got Spike on the Tuesday before Thanksgiving last fall.
- *titles of relatives when they are used as a name.*
  I can't have a cat because Mom and my sister have allergies.
- *names of places, buildings, and monuments.*
  I am taking care of the cats while Maggie and her family are on vacation in New York City. She is going to visit the Empire State Building and the Statue of Liberty.
- *direction words when they name a region.*
  We live in the Southeast. Maggie and her family flew north yesterday morning.

Find and correct 16 errors in capitalization in the paragraph below. Some words should be capitalized and some should not. Mark three lines under each letter that needs to be capitalized (i). Draw a line through each letter that should not be capitalized (✗).

The best time to visit Washington, D.c., is in the early spring. the weather is just right in april, not too hot or cold. The cherry blossoms were in bloom while we were there, so that made my Mom happy! We got to the Capital early monday morning after a ten-hour drive from the midwest. After checking into our hotel, we decided to visit the national Air and space Museum first. I could have spent all week there, although the Washington monument, the Lincoln Memorial, and the White house were really cool. I was hoping to see the president, but he was in europe. We did see a Senator from our State, though.

Write a complete sentence to answer each of the following questions. Use capital letters where necessary.

1. **In which region of the United States is your home state?**
   We live in the Northwest region.

2. **What two holidays do people celebrate during the tenth month of the year?**
   The two holidays we celebrate in october are "Colombus day" and Halloween.

3. **If you could have any pet, what would you choose and what would you name it?**
   I would have a pet dog and I would name it Beach.

Name _____

And the Winner Is . . .

As a writer, you need to know how to use commas to let readers know where to pause when reading a sentence.

Use a comma

- *after each item in a series of three or more, except after the last item.*
  Max wrote, read, and revised his story.
- *to set off the name of the person you are addressing directly.*
  Will you read it one more time, Jamie?
- *after introductory words like yes, no, and well.*
  Yes, I have some time right now.
- *to set off an appositive from the rest of the sentence.*
  The Pen to Paper Club, a writers' organization, sponsored a contest.
- *before a conjunction that joins two sentences.*
  Max entered his story, but he never thought he'd win.
- *after a dependent clause that begins a sentence.*
  When the letter came, Max was too nervous to open it.
- *to set off words that interrupt the basic idea of a sentence.*
  Max's sister, therefore, opened it for him.
- *to separate geographical names and dates.*
  Max won a trip to Orlando, Florida. They left Monday, June 23, 2003.

Write a sentence to answer each question. Include commas where they are needed.

1. **On what day and date will you celebrate your next birthday?**

My birthday is on January 12, so my next birthday is on 1/12/20.

2. **If you could choose to live in any city or town in any state, where would it be?**

I would live in Hawii, Honilule.

3. **How would you complete the following sentence?**

Whenever I sleep I, close my eyes.

4. **Imagine that you have been asked to introduce the President of the United States at a town hall meeting. How would you begin your introduction using direct address?**

Welcome to town hall Washington D.C.

5. **How would you use *and* in a sentence that tells what you had for lunch yesterday and what you had for lunch today?**

To day we had pizza for lunch, and yesterday we had macroni.

As you read a newspaper, your favorite magazine, a letter, or a book, look for five examples of commas in sentences and write them on a sheet of paper. Then identify the comma rule that was used.

Name _____

Listen to the Music

You can use the conjunctions and, but, and or to combine parts of sentences. When the subjects of two or more sentences share the same verb, you can combine them using and. Change the verb form from singular to plural if the subject is plural.

Kyle likes music. Jessie likes music.   Kyle and Jessie like music.

When the objects in two or more sentences are different but share the same subject and predicate, you can also combine them into one sentence.

Kyle enjoys jazz. He enjoys rock.   Kyle enjoys jazz and rock.
Kyle can play jazz. Kyle can play rock.   Kyle can play jazz and rock.

When the subjects of two or more sentences are the same but have different predicates, you can combine them into one sentence using and and sometimes but.

Kyle sings. He plays drums in a band.   Kyle sings and plays drums in a band.
Jessie plays guitar. Jessie doesn't sing.   Jessie plays guitar but doesn't sing.

Complete each pair of sentences. Then use the rules above to combine them.

1. Many songbirds eat ____Meat____. Many songbirds eat ____potatos____.
Many songbirds eat meat and potatos.

2. You should always ____Brush your teeth____ You should always ____Brush you hir____
You should always Brush you hair and teeth.

3. A ____Dime____ is worth less than a quarter. A ____penny____ is worth less than a quarter.
A Dime is worth less than a quater or a penny.

4. The ____Washington____ is a famous landmark. The ____Lincon____ is a famous landmark.
The Washington Momument and The Lincon Mumorial are famous Landmarks

5. All living things need ____Water____. All living things need ____food____.
All living things need water and food

6. ____Bears____ hibernate in winter. ____Other animals____ hibernate in winter.
Bears and other Animals hibrenate in winter.

7. Many kids enjoy ____No school____. Many kids enjoy ____Hollydays____.
Many kids enjoy No school and the Holidays.

8. The boys ____Play____ in the lake. The boys ____Swim____ in the lake.
The boys Play and swim in the lake.

 Look in a book, magazine, or newspaper for several sentences with compound subjects, compound predicates, or compound objects. Then show how they could be written as two or more short sentences. Compare. Which is more effective, the combined sentence or the short sentences?

That's Deep!

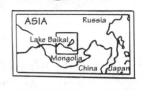

 *An **appositive** is a word or phrase that follows a noun or pronoun and explains or identifies what it is or gives more information about it. Commas set off an appositive from the rest of the sentence.*

Lake Baikal, the world's deepest lake, is in Siberia, a region of Russia.

If the subjects in two related sentences are the same, you can sometimes combine the sentences by using an appositive.

Sentence 1: **Baikal is also known as the world's oldest freshwater lake.**

Sentence 2: **It dates back about 25 million years.**

Combined: **Baikal, also known as the world's oldest freshwater lake, dates back about 25 million years.**

Underline two sentences in each paragraph that can be combined by using an appositive. Then write the combined sentence. Remember to include commas.

What is the world's most expensive spice? If you guessed saffron, then you are right. Saffron is worth about $2000 a pound. It takes a long time to harvest saffron. That is why it costs so much.

_____

_____

The atlas moth is the world's largest moth. It has a wingspan of about 12 inches. Picture a dinner plate, and you'll have a good idea about how large an atlas moth is. They are so large that people sometimes mistake them for birds when they are in flight. Atlas moths are found in tropical areas.

_____

_____

Georgia is the top peanut-producing state in the United States. It harvests over 2 billion pounds of peanuts each year. Georgia provides about half the peanuts used for making peanut butter. Did you know that our country's 39th president was also a peanut farmer in Plains, Georgia? Jimmy Carter served as president from 1977 to 1981.

_____

_____

Chocolate is popular throughout the world. Believe it or not, the average person in Switzerland eats about 19 pounds of chocolate per year! That is eight pounds more a year than the average American eats. In fact, Switzerland holds the world record. It is a small country to the north of Italy. As a country, the Swiss consume an annual total of about 138 million pounds of chocolate.

_____

_____

Rise and Shine

You can use **subordinate conjunctions** to combine sentences. These words, listed below, can show cause and effect and time relationships between the sentences you combine.

since   when   after   unless   because   as   while   before   if   although   until   whenever

The combined sentence will have two parts, an **independent clause** and a **dependent clause**.
If you put the dependent clause at the beginning of a sentence, follow it with a comma.

Amy fell asleep in class today. She had stayed up too late last night.

independent clause   dependent clause

Amy fell asleep in class today because she had stayed up too late last night.

The bell rang. Amy woke up and realized she had been asleep.

dependent clause   independent clause

When the bell rang, Amy woke up and realized she had been asleep.

Combine each pair of sentences. Use one of the subordinate conjunctions from above.

1. Miss Lee never said a word in class. She knew Amy had been asleep.

Miss Lee never said a word in class, because she knew
Amy had been asleep.

2. Amy was walking toward the door. Miss Lee called her name.

Amy was walking toward the door untill Miss Lee called her name.

3. Her face turned bright red. She was really embarrassed.

Her face turned bright red since she was really embarrassed.

4. Poor Amy tried to calm down. She turned and faced Miss Lee.

Poor Amy tried to calm down as she turned and faced MissLee

5. Jess and I waited just outside the door. Miss Lee spoke to Amy.

Jess and I waited Just outside the door until Miss Lee spoke to
Amy.

6. Amy explained why she had fallen asleep. She apologized to Miss Lee.

Amy explaned why she had fallen asleep after she apologized to
Miss Lee

7. We weren't sure if Amy was in trouble. She came out with a smile on her face.

We werent sure if Amy was in trouble since she came out with
a smile on her face.

8. We raced to our next class. Amy told us what Miss Lee said.

We raced to our next class while Amy told us what Miss Lee said

 Write a brief paragraph to explain what you think Miss Lee said to Amy. Use a subordinate conjunction in some of your sentences.

Time to Experiment

 Combining sentences helps to eliminate the problem of short or choppy sentences in paragraphs. You can often combine related sentences into compound sentences by using the conjunctions and, but, or, *and* so. *Compare the following two paragraphs and decide which is easier to understand.*

Young Alva was curious about everything. That curiosity led him to continually ask questions. His mother had been a teacher. She didn't always know the answers. If no one could tell him, he experimented. Once he wanted to know how hens hatch chickens. He put some eggs in a basket and sat on them. Can you guess who Alva is? Do you need another hint?

Young Alva was curious about everything, and that curiosity led him to continually ask questions. His mother had been a teacher, but she didn't always know the answers. If no one could tell him, he experimented. Once he wanted to know how hens hatch chickens, so he put some eggs in a basket and sat on them. Can you guess who Alva is, or do you need another hint?

Read the paragraph. Place parentheses around the pairs of sentences that can be combined with *and, but, or,* or *so.* Then rewrite the paragraph with the combined sentences. Remember to include commas.

My brother Alex has more "interests" than anyone I know. The novelty always wears off very quickly. I know my brother! Last week, Alex wanted to join the school band. He asked if he could rent a drum set. I burst out laughing. My parents just looked at each other. I knew what they were thinking. Would they be able to convince Alex to try something a little quieter? Would he insist on the drums? Well, they convinced Alex to try something else. It wasn't something quieter. Today he informed us that he's decided to try the tuba. In fact, the school has an extra tuba. Mom and Dad won't have to rent one. Needless to say, I hope this novelty wears off very, very, very quickly!

_____

_____

_____

_____

_____

_____

_____

_____

_____

_____

 Write another paragraph to continue the story. Tell what you think will happen. Include several compound sentences.

Solve the Problem

➡ *Sometimes you take the important details from several related sentences and combine them into one sentence to make the meaning of the sentences more clear. Compare the two paragraphs.*

    Seagulls can be a problem at the beach. I was trying to eat a sandwich when a gull landed near my blanket. <u>The bird was fearless. It snatched the sandwich out of my hand. It happened suddenly.</u> I couldn't believe it!

Notice how choppy the underlined three sentences are.

    Seagulls can be a problem at the beach. I was trying to eat a sandwich when a gull landed near my blanket. <u>The fearless bird suddenly snatched the sandwich right out of my hand.</u> I couldn't believe it!

By combining the information into one sentence, you can solve the problem of short, choppy sentences, improve your writing, and make the sentence more clear.

Read each paragraph. Put parentheses around the groups of sentences with details that can be combined into one sentence. Look for other ways to combine sentences as well. Then rewrite the paragraph with the changes.

    What a summer I spent! It was fantastic. It was at the shore. I spent it with my grandparents. They have a summer home. It is near Cape May. That is in New Jersey. We went swimming. We collected shells. We fished. Their house is right on the beach. We never had to go far. The beach was my backyard. It was great.

_____

_____

_____

_____

_____

    My grandfather has a motorboat. It is small. It is called a runabout. He keeps it at a marina. The marina is nearby. Gramps took me crabbing one morning. It was before sunrise. I was half asleep. My job was tying fish heads to the lines. The fish heads were smelly. That sure woke me up. It was worth it. We caught crabs. They were blue. We caught six dozen. What a great dinner we had that night!

_____

_____

_____

_____

_____

Powerful Paragraphs

*A **paragraph** is a group of sentences that focuses on a topic and one main idea about that topic. A **topic sentence** expresses that main idea. It may answer who, what, where, when, why, how, or a combination of questions. Although a topic sentence often begins a paragraph, it can come at the end or even in the middle of a paragraph. The other sentences in the paragraph develop the main idea by telling more about it. They are called **supporting sentences**.*

Read each paragraph. Underline the topic sentence in each one. Put parentheses around each supporting sentence. Then write the question or questions that each topic sentence answers.

There is an energizing chill in the air now that the days are shorter. The last of the crops are about to be harvested, and a blanket of leaves covers much of the landscape. All but a few of our summertime visitors have already flown south for warmer places. Once again, the long, hot days of summer have given way to fall.

_____

_____

_____

Falling asleep was never a problem for me until we moved to the country. I was used to the sounds of subway trains pulling into the station near our apartment, the horns and squealing brakes of buses, taxis, and cars, wailing sirens, and planes landing or taking off. I was not used to the sound of chirping crickets. My parents assured me that I would get used to it. They were right, of course, but it took awhile.

_____

_____

_____

This amazing marsupial spends up to 22 hours a day asleep in a eucalyptus tree. A nocturnal creature, it is mostly active at night. The habits of the world's sleepiest animal, the koala, really fascinate me. When it is awake, the koala feeds on eucalyptus leaves and shoots, up to two pounds at a time. What's more, it seldom drinks water because it gets most of what it needs from the leaves and shoots.

_____

_____

_____

12-28-2019

Grab Some Attention

A **topic sentence** expresses the main idea about the topic of a paragraph. It should tell just enough to interest your readers. Remember that it may answer who, what, where, when, why, or how, or a combination of questions. Here is an example.

Topic: **an accident on a space station**

Topic Sentence: **An alarm shattered the silence, alerting the crew that something was terribly wrong.**

Here are some topics. For each one, write a topic sentence that would grab the attention of your readers.

1. Topic: a frightening experience

   Topic Sentence: _____

2. Topic: wearing uniforms to school, yes or no

   Topic Sentence: _____

3. Topic: a brush fire that burned out of control

   Topic Sentence: _____

4. Topic: why the opossum has no hair on its tail

   Topic Sentence: _____

5. Topic: witnessing a friend steal a candy bar

   Topic Sentence: _____

Now come up with some topics of your own. Then write a topic sentence for each one.

6. Topic: _Opening a present That you did not want_

   Topic Sentence: _Ripp, Ripp, Rripp, ... Nooooooo!_

7. Topic: _I Got a bad grade on a test._

   Topic Sentence: _Oh no my perents are going to kill me._

8. Topic: _Decorating a Christmas Tree_

   Topic Sentence: _I wiped the Lights, climed the tree for the star, and the rowded the Ordevents._

9. Topic: _Puppet show_

   Topic Sentence: _I sit down Looking and Laphing at the puppets._

Keep a writer's journal or small notebook handy. Whenever you get an idea for a topic, jot it down. Then write some possible topic sentences.

12-28-2019

The Mighty End

 No matter what your purpose for writing—to inform, persuade, or entertain—or what form your writing takes—story, news report, explanation, letter to an editor, or personal narrative—try to include a strong ending sentence. The ending sentence in a paragraph is called the **closing sentence**. *It retells the topic sentence in a new way. It can be a surprise or an unexpected solution. It can ask a question or answer a question. It can explain or teach something. Here are some examples.*

Nothing else could possibly go wrong . . . could it?
Top your sundae with fresh whipped cream and a cherry, and enjoy!
Aren't you glad you didn't live back then?
To this day, the mystery of the disappearing statue has never been solved.
That's what they told us, but we knew better!
Thanksgiving will always be my favorite family gathering.
So, be careful what you wish for because it just may happen.
Would you want to eat at that restaurant?
Unfortunately, we still had three more hours to go!

Write a strong closing sentence for each writing situation below.

1. **a news report about an earthquake or tornado**

The earth stoped shaking and the tornado stoped soon and every thing is ok now.

2. **an account of a UFO sighting**

We still can not find the UFO, but we will find it soon. that is [illegible] now force

3. **an explanation of how to study for a history test**

That is how you study for a History test →

4. **an ad for a nutritious cereal you have developed**

That is why I love it

5. **a warning about skateboarding without the proper equipment**

don't do that kids because that is all.

6. **a lesson on how to make the perfect submarine sandwich**

And that is how it's done.

7. **a letter of apology to a friend for something you have done**

I am sorry —Love your friend Kayor

8. **an account of an embarrassing moment**

That is why I never want Leave home

9. **a story about camping in the woods**

[illegible] Be warm and Have fun. The end

 Now choose one of your sentences. Then develop and write a paragraph on a sheet of paper with a beginning and a middle that leads to an ending that concludes with your sentence.

In the Know

You know that a paragraph should have a topic sentence that expresses
the main idea of the paragraph. Here is a topic sentence from a story.

**Malcolm could never have imagined the incredible journey he
was about to make.**

*Who is Malcolm? Where will his journey take him? Is it to a real place
or to some imaginary place? Why is it incredible? What will happen?
Whom will he meet?*

*These are just a few of the questions you may ask after reading the
topic sentence. You can use the answers to questions like these to
develop supporting details for the paragraphs you write.*

Read each topic sentence. Write the questions you would want the paragraph to answer.

**1. So faint was the sound of it that Emerald thought it was just the rustling of leaves stirred
by the gentle breeze.**

_____

_____

_____

2. Maggie realized that there was only one way to end the ridiculous argument.

_____

_____

_____

3. Max thought baking a birthday cake was a "piece of cake," but he was wrong!

_____

_____

_____

**4. They're fun to ride, they're completely portable, and millions of kids ride them
every day.**

_____

_____

_____

5. SSSSSSTHUNKITTYTHUNKITTYTHUNK! "What now?" moaned Andreas.

_____

_____

_____

Name _____

Choose and rewrite one of the topic sentences on page 20. Then reread the questions you listed and use your imagination to answer them. Use your answers to write supporting sentences for a possible paragraph. Add any other details that you think of to support the topic.

Topic Sentence: _____

_____

Supporting Sentences:

- _____

_____

- _____

_____

- _____

_____

- _____

_____

- _____

_____

Now, use the information to write a paragraph. Include a closing sentence. Remember to indent, capitalize, and punctuate correctly.

_____

_____

_____

_____

_____

_____

_____

_____

_____

 Illustrate your story. Then share it with someone you know.

A Scrumptious Topic

Before you write a first draft of a paragraph, take the time to think about the topic and to review the facts, details, and ideas you have written.

Read the topic and the notes for a paragraph about the world's best hot fudge sundae. Cross out the details which seem unnecessary or unrelated. Then read the three possible topic sentences. Make a check next to the best topic sentence.

Topic: the world's best hot fudge sundae

Details: at least 3 scoops of vanilla ice cream, should fill bowl—a big bowl
mounds of fresh-whipped heavy cream—slightly sweetened
need napkins
big spoonful or 2 or 3 spoons of chopped walnuts
lots and lots of hot fudge, has to be thick and gooey
a couple of cherries on top with a little cherry juice
hot, cold, sweet, crunchy, smooth, creamy, yummy all in one
meant to be shared with a friend—or not
don't forget the spoon
perfect dessert for ice cream lovers—young and old
serve with a glass of water

Possible topic sentences:
There is absolutely nothing more scrumptious than my hot fudge sundae recipe.
The hardest part of making a hot fudge sundae is not eating it as you make it.
If you like ice cream, you'll love my recipe for a hot fudge sundae.

Number the details above to show the order in which you would use them. The order should make sense. Then use the details to write supporting sentences in order below.

_____
_____
_____
_____
_____
_____
_____
_____

 Use the topic sentence and supporting sentences to write a paragraph on another sheet of paper.

Name _____

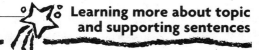

Now, choose one of the following topics, or one of your own, and follow the steps.

friendship	**making a BLT on toast**	**a great hobby**
sunset	**a national political figure**	**a mystery gift**
a superstition	**a musical instrument**	**a current event**

- Write the topic and list at least five details or facts about it.
- Review your list. Cross out any facts or details that do not relate to the topic. Add any other details that are important. Number the details in an order that makes sense.
- Write several possible topic sentences. Check the one that best tells the main idea.

Topic: _____

Details:

_____

_____

_____

_____

Possible topic sentences:

_____

_____

_____

Write a first draft. Begin by writing the topic sentence that best tells the main idea. Then use the numbered facts and details to write sentences that support your topic sentence.

_____

_____

_____

_____

_____

Now proofread your first draft. Do the sentences support the topic sentence? Are they in an order that makes sense? Are they clearly written and interesting? Do they begin and end correctly? Revise your paragraph. Make the necessary changes. Then rewrite the paragraph on another sheet of paper.

 Using the paragraph you just completed, write each sentence on a separate strip of paper. Mix up the sentence strips. Then challenge someone to put the sentences in the correct order.

12-27-2019

Read Carefully

When you **proofread** your work, you look for errors and mark them so that you can correct them. Here are some marks you can use when you proofread your work.

delete	The the phone rang.
insert a word	The ʌphone rang.
insert a comma	The phone rang ʌand I answered it.
insert quotation marks	A voice said, "Hello."
insert a period	The phone rang ⊙
insert an apostrophe	Its ringing again.
close up space	The ph one rang.
insert a space	The phone rang.
switch order of letters	The phone ragn.
capitalize	the phone rang.
make lowercase	The pHone rang.
start new paragraph	¶ The phone rang.

Read the following part of a story. Proofread it using the marks above. There are 13 errors.

The most amazing thing happened this morning. I still can't believe it! Just as I was about to fill one of my feeders, I noticed a Chickadee perched on the lower branch of a nearby tree. The little bird seemed to be watching me. Of course, chickadees really like like sunflower seeds and that's what I always put in this feeder. I figured it was probably hungry and just waiting for me to finish up and leave. It was then that I got this great idea.

Chicadees are supposed to be easy to hand tame. well, the chickadee was still perched on the, and I had the seeds, so I decided to try. I took a bunch of seeds, held out my hand—palm up—next to the feeder and stood very still. I didnt even scra tch my nose when it started to itch! About a minute later, the chickadee flew to the tree closest to the feeder. I held my breath and waited. The didn't fly to my hand, but it did fly to the feeder! It took a seed and flew off to eat it. I knew it wuold be back, so I continued to watch and wait.

Pretend you are the storyteller. Write another paragraph to tell what happened when the chickadee came back. Then proofread your writing. Use the marks at the top of the page.

12-27-2014

Working Together

 Illustrations and photographs often contain important and interesting details that you can use to write a story, an article, an essay, or just a simple paragraph.

Study the photo. Think about the details it shows and what you can write about.

Write a possible topic sentence for the photo.

We are cleaning the neighborhood garden to help our community.

Write as many details as you can about the photo that support the topic sentence.

A small park with people picking up trash, two guys picking up trash
one boy holding wood and two girls sweeping. In a small open city space
in a big ally. A big retangal space. A small city park, with no care, untill
today.

Review your ideas. Then write a brief paragraph about the scene in the photo. Include a
closing sentence.

A small park with people helping to keep it clean. Two guys picking
up trash, one boy holding wood, one girl raking out leaves, and
another girl holding a sign. They are cleaning a smallish retangal
space, that had no care, untill today. They are cleaning the neighborhood
garden for our community.

 **Find and cut out a magazine photo of a scenic location you would like to visit. This time, use the
photo to come up with ideas for an advertisement, an article for a travel magazine, or a paragraph
about the dream vacation you are planning.**

Name _____ 12-27-2019

Make It Exact

 You can make your writing more interesting, exciting, and colorful by choosing and replacing dull, overused, or inexact words.

Big waves hit the land along the sea during the storm.
Gigantic waves battered the coast during the hurricane.

Keep a thesaurus handy when you write and revise your writing.

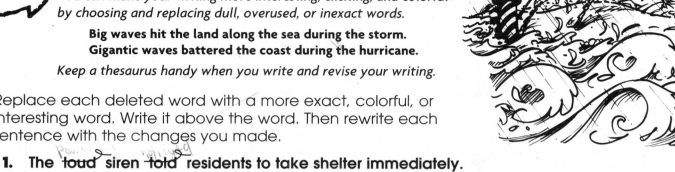

Replace each deleted word with a more exact, colorful, or interesting word. Write it above the word. Then rewrite each sentence with the changes you made.

1. The ~~loud~~ siren ~~told~~ residents to take shelter immediately.
   The powerful siren notifyed residents to take shelter immediantely.

2. The ~~tired~~ hikers nearly collapsed after the ~~hard~~ trek.
   The draind hikers, nearly collapsed after the rough trek.

3. My opponent may be ~~small~~, but what a ~~strong~~ serve she delivers!
   My opponent may be short, but what a active serve she delivers!

4. What is the name of that ~~bright~~ blue bird ~~sitting~~ on the feeder?
   What is the name of that dazziling blue bird sitting on the feeder

5. The men ~~stopped~~ as the rattler ~~moved~~ across their path.
   The men blocked as the rattle lifted across their path.

6. The audience ~~laughed~~ at the comedian's ~~funny~~ stories.
   The audience giggled at the comedian's ridiculous stories.

7. What is that ~~bad~~ odor ~~coming~~ from the kitchen?
   What is that awful odor, heading from the kitchen?

8. Look how the limbs on that ~~tall~~ oak are ~~moving~~ in the wind.
   Look how the limbs on that towering oak are lifted in the wind.

9. It took an hour to ~~move~~ the heavy ~~load~~ up the steep incline.
   It took an hour to act the heavy amount up the steep incline.

10. What an interesting ~~story~~ the survivors told their ~~surprised~~ rescuers!
    What an intresting book the survivors told their astounished rescuers!

 Just for fun, rewrite a familiar children's story such as "Little Red Riding Hood" for an older audience. Look for dull, overused, and inexact words and replace them with more interesting, exciting, and colorful words. For example, you might change "Grandmother, what big ears you have!" said Little Red Riding Hood to "Grandmother, what enormous ears you have!" exclaimed Petite Crimson Riding Hood.

It's All Business!

There are many reasons for writing a business letter. You might request information, express an opinion to a public official, or explain a problem with something you have bought. A business letter has six parts.

The **heading** *gives your address and the date.*

The **inside address** *gives the name and address of the person or company receiving the letter. It can include the person's title.*

A **formal greeting,** *such as* Dear Sir:, *comes next. It can include a title of respect, such as Mr., Mrs., or Ms.*

The **body** *states the purpose of your letter.*

A **formal closing,** *such as* Sincerely yours, *follows the body.*

Your **signature** *is last.*

Imagine that you ordered the Thingamabob, a popular new toy from the Razzle-Dazzle Toy Company, for $29.99. It was a gift for your younger brother. Unfortunately, the toy broke the first time he played with it! How would you feel? Would you want your money back? Would you want another Thingamabob? Write a letter to Mr. Dewey Cheatem, the president of the company at 123 Any Street, Anytown, Anystate, 00001. Explain why you are writing. Tell what happened and how. Then suggest a solution to the problem.

heading → 3427 Kettmann RD
C.A. San Jose, 95121

123 Any street,   ← inside address
Any town, Any state,
00001

Dear Mr. Dewey Cheatem,: ← formal greeting

body
↓
There is some prodlem with the "Thingamabob" toy I got. It did not work, also one of the lags broke off. It stopped shaking and bouncing. I would request a new made one for exchange or a refund.

formal closing → Thank you for your time,
signature → Raynik

Name _____

12-28-19

Using facts and opinions to persuade

The Power of Persuasion

 Have you ever tried to convince someone to feel the way you do about something? To write a convincing **persuasive paragraph**, *state your opinion clearly, give reasons, and support your opinion with facts. Remember that facts can be checked or proven. Here is an example from a letter to the editor of a newspaper.*

Our town should consider building a skateboard park. According to a recent community survey, there are more kids skateboarding than ever before but fewer places to skateboard. Certain townspeople and merchants have complained to authorities that skateboarders make too much noise, create a nuisance for pedestrians and drivers, and are causing property damage. As a result, we skateboarders are continually "asked" to move on. We are always looking for new places to practice. Specially designated areas and parks for skateboarders have worked in other communities with similar problems. If everyone would work together, it could work here.

Jason Anderson

Green Hills

Answer each question about the letter to the editor above.

1. **What opinion does Jason state in his letter?** _They want more skate parks._

2. **What reasons does Jason give?** _More people are skating now, it is causing problems because there is not a lot of skate parks._

3. **What facts does Jason present to support his opinion?** _People think the skate boarders are causing to much noise, property damge and more._

Think about some problems and issues that affect your school, neighborhood, community, or state. Choose one that you feel deeply about. What is your opinion? Write what you think should be done to resolve the problem or issue.

I think to just bild it for them because so they dont darther you any more.

List reasons for your opinion.

If you just bild it for them hopfuly they will leave every one alown and noone gets barthered. Skate parks are not just for skateboads.

List facts to support your opinion.

every one can have fun and not barther you.

_____

_____

 Now, write a paragraph on another sheet of paper. Then ask friends to read your paragraph and share their responses. Do they agree or disagree with you? Why? Do they have suggestions that could improve your paragraph to make it more persuasive? Revise your paragraph.

12-28-18

Name _____

Step by Step

 *Whenever you write about something that has happened or how to do or to make something,
it is important to write about the events or the steps in the correct order.*

Carefully read the notes about the day the Mason family went on vacation.
Number the events in the order that they happened

- **8** back on road by 1:00
- **7** stopped for lunch around noon
- **1** helped Dad load up the van
- **10** unloaded van and went down to the beach
- **1** up at 6:00 A.M., got dressed, ate breakfast
- **3** double-checked house before locking up
- **5** stopped for gas on way out of town
- **9** arrived at the motel by late afternoon
- **6** got on the turnpike and headed east
- **4** piled in the van and ready to go by 7:30

Pretend that the notes above are yours. Use them to write a paragraph. Include a topic
sentence, closing sentence, and title. Write about the events in sequence. Remember to
indent the first line and to begin and end each sentence correctly. You may want to include
words such as *before that, after, first, next, then, later,* and *finally* to help indicate the order
in which you did things. Use another sheet of paper, if needed.

Going to the Beach

First, at 6:00 am in the morning I got dressed and ate breakfast. My mom
my sister and I helped dad load the van. Second, we made sure we got every
thing before we locked up the house. We were ready to go by 7:30. On our way
out of town we stopped for gas. Then we headed east. Third, we stopped for lunch,
then got back on the road by 1:00. Later, we arrived at the the motel.
We un loaded the van and went down to the beach. That was the
day I spent with my family at the beach.

💡 **Think about something that you know how to do or make. Write the steps in the process. Then use
your notes to tell someone about it.**

Finding the Way

 *A **how-to paragraph** gives directions for doing or making something. It usually includes a topic sentence, the necessary materials, and step-by-step directions. A writer often uses time order words and phrases such as* first, next, then, after that, *and* finally *to help indicate the sequence. A how-to paragraph can also give directions for getting from one place to another. Here is a paragraph in which the directions are not very clear.*

Do you turn left or right at the light?   How many blocks are "a few" blocks?   Which street?

Getting from school to my house is a snap. Just walk a few blocks down the street toward town. Turn at the traffic light. Go a couple more blocks. My house is on the corner. If you go past the intersection, you've gone too far.

Which intersection is too far?   How many blocks are "a couple more" blocks?   Which corner?

How would you give directions to get from one place to another in your community, such as from your home to the mall, from your school to a certain store, or from the park to the library? To get started, close your eyes and picture the route as if you were actually walking. Sketch the route in the box below. Then write a how-to paragraph with clear and specific directions. Include the names of streets and buildings, direction words such as *left*, *right*, *north*, *south*, *east*, and *west*, and time-order words.

```



```

From _____ **to** _____

_____

_____

_____

_____

_____

_____

Definitely Dynamic

*Writing a **definition paragraph** is similar to defining a word in your own terms, only it is much more inclusive and personal. You not only define the word, but you include details that answer some these questions: What is it like? What is it not like? Why is it important? What purpose does it serve? Where or when do you use it? What does it look like? Does it make or have a sound? What kind of sound does it make or have? What does it feel like? Does it have a taste? How? Does it smell? How? What does it do? What doesn't it do? Does it make you feel a certain way? How? What do others think or feel about it?*

List several common nouns. Here are a few to get you started.

friendship	sneakers	_____	_____
pencil	hamburger	_____	_____
helmet	key	_____	_____
onion	skateboard	_____	_____
home	happiness	_____	_____

Choose three words. Look up each one in a dictionary and write the definition.

_____ : _____

_____ : _____

_____ : _____

Now, write a short definition paragraph for one of the words that not only tells what it is but also includes details that answer some of the questions above. Remember to include a topic sentence and a closing sentence. Use your imagination and creativity.

_____

_____

_____

_____

_____

_____

_____

_____

Read and Review

A **book review** *is one way to share a book you have read. It has three parts—an introduction, a body, and a conclusion—and includes facts and opinions supported by reasons. The* **introduction** *is a paragraph that begins with an attention-grabbing topic sentence. The* **body** *includes a summary of the plot and information about the setting and main characters. It can be more than one paragraph. The* **conclusion** *can include a hint about the ending and your opinions and reading recommendations. Before writing a review, it helps to write facts about the book and your opinions and reasons.*

Choose a novel you have recently read. Fill in the book-review planner.

Facts

Title: _____ Author: _____

Type of Book (science fiction, realistic fiction, mystery, etc.): _____

Main Character(s): _____

_____

Setting (where, when): _____

Plot (main events, problem/solution): _____

_____

Special Features (illustrations/photographs, language, diary/journal entries): _____

_____

Opinions

The character(s) I liked most and why: _____

How I would describe the plot—interesting, exciting, boring, so-so—and why: _____

_____

The part of the book I enjoyed most (least) and why: _____

_____

Features of the book I liked (disliked) and why:_____

_____

Why I would (would not) recommend this book: _____

_____

Now use the information you recorded to write a book review. Remember to include facts and opinions.

Name _____

A Great Way to Organize

*An **outline** is a great way to organize facts and ideas when you are getting ready to write a piece with two or more paragraphs. Each main idea becomes a paragraph with a topic sentence expressing the main idea. Facts and details listed under each main idea are used in sentences to support the main idea.*

Suppose you are writing your autobiography—the story of your life. Use the outline form below. For numerals I, II, and III, list details that tell about each main idea listed. For numeral IV, come up with another possible main idea, such as important influences, major events, facts about your family, or influential people, and then list details.

All About Me → **main topic**

I. **Biographical Facts** → **Main Idea 1**

   A. _____ **facts and details**

   B. _____

   C. _____

   D. _____

II. **My Earliest Memories** → **Main Idea 2**

   A. _____ **facts and details**

   B. _____

   C. _____

   D. _____

III. **My Major Accomplishments** → **Main Idea 3**

   A. _____ **facts and details**

   B. _____

   C. _____

   D. _____

IV. _____ → **Main Idea 4**

   A. _____ **facts and details**

   B. _____

   C. _____

   D. _____

Now use your outline to write your autobiography.

Getting Organized

When you are getting ready to write two or more
paragraphs for a report, you can make the task easier
if you follow these steps:

• *Organize related facts and details into groups.*

• *Write a topic sentence expressing the main idea
for each group.*

• *Use the facts and details in each group to write
sentences that support each topic sentence.*

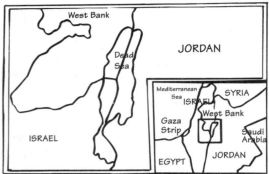

The Dead Sea is a saltwater lake located between Israel and Jordan. Read the facts and
organize them into three groups for a report. Think of a category name for each group of
facts. Then use ✱s, ✔s, and ✕s to indicate the facts that belong in each group.

✱ = _____

✔ = _____

✕ = _____

_____ 1. one of the saltiest bodies of water in world

_____ 2. covers about 400 square miles

_____ 3. almost impossible for swimmers to sink in Dead Sea because of
high density of salt

_____ 4. water comes from Jordan River and streams

_____ 5. measures about 11 miles wide at widest point

_____ 6. water so salty that fish die immediately; nothing but
simple microorganisms survive in Dead Sea

_____ 7. measures about 31 miles long

_____ 8. its shore lowest place on surface of Earth

_____ 9. bottom measures to depths of 2,622 feet below sea level

_____ 10. water doesn't flow out of Dead Sea

_____ 11. water evaporates, leaving salt and other minerals behind

On the following page, write a topic sentence for each group of facts. Then use the facts to
write sentences that support each topic sentence.

**Find and read an article on another geographic location. Record a group of facts about the location.
Then divide the facts into categories.**

Name _____

Subject: **The Dead Sea**

Topic Sentence for Paragraph 1: _____

_____

Supporting Sentences:

_____

_____

_____

_____

_____

_____

Topic Sentence for Paragraph 2: _____

_____

Supporting Sentences:

_____

_____

_____

_____

_____

_____

Topic Sentence for Paragraph 3: _____

_____

Supporting Sentences:

_____

_____

_____

_____

_____

Use all the information to write a report about the Dead Sea on another sheet of paper.

The Narrator

Every story, or **narrative**, *has a narrator. When you choose to tell a story from a first-person point of view, the narrator is a story character who uses the pronouns* I, me, *and* myself *to tell what he or she thinks, feels, and does. The readers see the story through the eyes of this character only.*

I tried to calm myself after looking down and seeing a scorpion crawling up my leg. I was terrified. "Matt," I croaked, barely able to speak, "please help me!" Matt turned around and raced to my side.

When you choose to tell a story from a third-person point of view, the narrator is not a character but rather someone outside the story. Your narrator reveals the actions and words of all the characters but tells the thoughts and feelings of only one main character.

She tried to calm herself after looking down and seeing a scorpion crawling up her leg. She was terrified. "Matt," she croaked, barely able to speak, "please help me!" Matt turned around and raced to her side.

Rewrite the following passage from a first-person point of view.

Spotting the doe in a clearing, he froze in his tracks and quietly took out his camera. He didn't want to startle the animal before getting at least one shot. Sensing his presence, the doe looked up at him. "Don't be frightened," he said in his most soothing voice. "I won't hurt you. I just want to take your picture." The doe accommodated him for about five seconds before running off into the woods.

_____

_____

_____

_____

Rewrite the following passage from a third-person point of view.

After hiking for more than an hour up the steep trail, I decided to take a break because my feet were killing me. Although I had worn my new hiking boots around the house all week, I soon realized that they were not sufficiently broken in. "I should have listened to Beth and worn my old boots," I grumbled to myself.
"Did you say something, Jenny?" Beth asked.

_____

_____

_____

_____

Name _____

Writing from different points of view

Look at the scenario below. Write a short story using the first-person point of view—either the camper's or the skunk's. A topic sentence is provided to help you get started.

It was an absolutely perfect summer evening at the Pine Grove Campgrounds until my

unexpected encounter _____

_____

_____

_____

_____

_____

_____

Now, rewrite the story using the third-person point of view.

It was an absolutely perfect summer evening at the Pine Grove Campgrounds until the

unexpected encounter _____

_____

_____

_____

_____

_____

_____

 Choose a favorite fairy tale such as "Little Red Riding Hood," "Goldilocks and the Three Bears," or "Jack and the Beanstalk." For fun, rewrite the story as a first-person narrative as if you were one of the characters.

Scholastic Success With Writing • Grade 5   37

Copyright © Scholastic Inc.

12-30-2019

Make a Plan

Before you write a story, it helps to plan. When you plan, you determine possible characters in your story, the setting (where and when the story takes place), and the plot (all the actions or events in the story). The plot includes a problem, events leading to the climax, or most exciting part of the story, and events leading to the resolution.

What kinds of stories do you like? Do you prefer historical fiction or realistic fiction, action adventures or mysteries, fairy tales or tall tales? Plan a story that you think your friends will enjoy. Use the answers to the questions below to plan your story.

What is the title? _The tit ____ Vit _li A Mystory In Crime_

Where will the story take place? _Home, Crime sean, School, wharhouse, jail, palece station_

When will the story take place? _A big house in 3519_

Who is the main character? _Violet Volpina_

What is the main character like? _She is a 6th grader, Detective, Lie detector, Bad girl_

What problem or problems will your main character face? _A bad guy, her family_ Tom Boy

What other characters will you include? _Stana (friend), Mom, sister, Winter (A bad guy) (Teacher) Ms. Apple gate,_

What will be the most exciting moment or turning point? _The bad guy chace._

What events or actions will lead up to this moment? _running ony her mornig Jog, Sees the bad guy then chases him._

What events or actions will follow this moment and show how the problem is resolved? _Violet will put Winter behind doars_

What is the resolution? _Violet finds out how speshel she is._

Will you tell your story in the first-person or third-person point of view? _Thind_

Now, review your plan. Make any revisions. Then write a draft of your story on another sheet of paper. Begin by writing a topic sentence that will grab the attention of your readers.

Time to Talk

 When you include dialogue in a story, use quotation marks around the speaker's exact words. Use a comma to set off the quotation from the rest of the sentence. Place end punctuation marks and commas inside the quotation marks.

Ben grumbled, "I can't find my sneakers."
"You're always misplacing something," commented his sister Maggie.

If a quotation is a question, end it with a question mark. If a quotation is an exclamation, end it with an exclamation mark.

"Where did you take them off?" asked Mrs. Abbot, trying to be helpful.
"Just follow the smell!" teased his brother.

If a quotation is divided but still one sentence, use commas to separate the quote from the words that tell who the speaker is.

"You may think you're a comedian," replied Ben, "but you're not funny."

If a quotation is divided and two separate sentences, place a period after the words that identify the speaker. Then begin the second sentence with a capital letter.

"I'm sorry," Sam apologized. "Your sneakers are on the back porch."

Read the following part of a story. Add the missing quotation marks, commas, and end punctuation.

It was Saturday morning, and Maggie was already in the kitchen.

Breakfast will be ready in about five minutes Maggie yelled up to her brothers

Do you want some help offered Mom, who had just walked into the kitchen

Thanks, Mom replied Maggie but I'd really like to do it myself

Okay agreed Mom I'll just take the dog for a quick walk then.

Maggie popped the bread into the toaster and went back to the stove to check on

the eggs and bacon

About a minute later, Ben said to Sam Do you smell something burning

Yup answered Sam It smells like burnt toast to me, and there goes the smoke alarm

I guess Maggie's making breakfast again laughed Ben, as they ran down to the

kitchen

Do you want some help, Maggie Ben and Sam asked.

On another sheet of paper, continue the story and the conversation between Ben, Sam, and Maggie. Begin by writing what Maggie said to her brothers. Try to include at least four quotations. Remember to indent each time a new person speaks.

 Read a page of a story or book with dialogue. Identify each rule the writer used for quotation marks, commas, and end punctuation.

12-30-2019

The Tone of Talk

When you include dialogue in your writing, do you usually use said *to signal the words of your speakers? You can make your writing more interesting and effective with words other than* said. *Compare the two versions of the same dialogue.*

"I'm tired," said Benny.
"Are we almost there?" said Lisa.
"It'll be another hour," Dad said.
"Okay," said Benny and Lisa.

"I'm tired," whined Benny.
"Are we almost there?" grumbled Lisa.
"It'll be another hour," Dad promised.
"Okay," sighed Benny and Lisa.

The words whined, grumbled, promised, *and* sighed *indicate the feelings and tone of voice of the speakers and make the dialogue more interesting to read.*

Read each sentence. List the feelings of each speaker. Consider each speaker's words and the word that signaled them.

1. "Silence!" bellowed Dad. ___"Silence!" Anger___

2. "That wasn't my intention," admitted Lisa. ___"Admitted" Sorry___

3. "What was that?" the child whispered. ___"Whispered" scared___

4. "It's not that difficult," my friend assured me. ___"assured" talking___

5. "Please be careful," warned my mother. ___"warned" worried___

6. "It's been a long, exhausting day," she yawned. ___"Yawned" tired___

7. "I can't believe you guys!" Jody chuckled. ___"chuckled" Happy___

Read the incomplete dialogue. Think about the word that signals each speaker's words. Then write what you think each speaker said.

   My brother Mikey is three years younger than I am, but he always wants to tag along with me.

"___I want to go to!___," insisted Mikey.

"___No___," I muttered, as I tried to leave without getting into an argument.

"___Yes I will___," he countered, grabbing his baseball glove.

"___Come On!___," I yelled, walking toward my bike.

"___What___," interrupted Mom.

"___But I don't Want Mikey I come___," I explained.

"___I will come with you___," complained Mikey.

"___Come bring miky with you now___," suggested Mom.

   I smiled at Mom and replied, "___Okay Come we will go now___." Then I looked over at Mikey who was now pouting and promised, "___I will be good___."

Name _____

Look back at page 40. Underline all the words that were used in place of *said*. Here are more words you can use. Think about what each might indicate about the feelings of a speaker or a speaker's tone of voice. Then complete each dialogue below by adding a word that you think best signals each speaker's words.

accused	giggled	persuaded	sobbed
argued	groaned	pleaded	squeaked
balked	hesitated	predicted	stuttered
blubbered	hissed	proposed	tattled
bragged	instructed	proposed	teased
consoled	joked	quoted	urged
corrected	laughed	repeated	wailed
demanded	mumbled	reported	whimpered
exclaimed	objected	roared	wondered
gasped	ordered	scolded	yelped

"Don't be too obvious, but check out that boy in the blue jacket," _____

Jackie to her friends. "He just took a magazine and stuffed it inside his jacket."

"I didn't see him do it," _____ Beth.

"Me either," _____ Jessica.

"You really should tell the store manager," _____ Mattie.

"I don't know," _____ Jackie. **"What do you think, Jessica?"**

"You don't have to do anything," she _____.

"It looks like someone else saw him and reported it."

"Have you ever seen anything so incredible?" _____ Ben.

"There must be thousands of them," he _____ , pointing to

the cloud of monarch butterflies flying overhead.

"There are," _____ his grandfather.

"Where are they going?" _____ Ben.

"Every fall," _____ Ben's grandfather, **"millions**

of monarchs migrate from Canada and parts of the United States

to Mexico for the winter. Some travel up to 2,000 miles."

"Wow!" _____ Ben.

Now think up a scenario of your own. Then write a conversation between two or three characters on another sheet of paper. Remember to indent each time a new character speaks.

Grab Some Interest

You can often expand a simple paragraph in a story, article, essay, report, or whatever you are writing and make it more interesting by

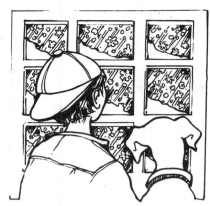

- *combining short, choppy sentences.*
- *adding details to help create a picture, mood, or feeling.*
- *replacing dull, overused, or inexact nouns, verbs, and adjectives.*
- *changing the order of words in sentences.*
- *adding words or phrases such as* also, first, meanwhile, in fact, however, eventually, *and* in the end *to connect ideas or events.*

Expand and rewrite each of the paragraphs using some of the suggestions above.

It was dusk. The snow began to fall. I was surprised. It was the end of April. Snow is unusual then. The temperature had fallen. That was earlier. Clouds began moving in. I knew a storm was coming. Would it be a snowstorm? I woke up the next morning. Snow covered the ground. There would be no baseball practice today!

_____

_____

_____

_____

_____

Something smelled good. We had just passed the bakery. We looked at each other. We smiled. We headed back to the bakery. Maggie opened the door. We went inside. What a sight! There were all kinds of goodies. There were breads and rolls. Some were just out of the oven. I went from case to case. Everything looked and smelled good. It was a hard decision. Finally, I chose.

_____

_____

_____

_____

_____

Find a storybook for young children in which the sentences and paragraphs are very simple. Then rewrite the book for students who are your age.

Figuratively Speaking

 Figurative language can be used to add details to sentences, to clarify a point, or to enhance your writing. **Metaphors, similes, hyperbole,** *and* **personification** *are four kinds of figurative language.*

A **simile** *makes a comparison between two unlike things, using* like *or* as.
Simon was mad as a hornet after discovering his bike had been stolen.

A **metaphor** *makes a comparison between two unlike things, without using* like *or* as.
The fog was a thick gray blanket covering the entire valley.

A **personification** *gives human characteristics and qualities to nonhuman things like animals and objects.*
The moon peeked through the clouds and smiled down on us.

A **hyperbole** *is a deliberate exaggeration.*
The tension was so thick you could cut it with a knife.

Complete each sentence with a simile, metaphor, hyperbole, or personification. Try to use each type of figurative language at least two times. Write S, M, P, or H before each sentence to label each figure of speech.

_____ **1.** Everyone was so exhausted by the end of the day that _____

_____

_____ **2.** Slowly meandering through the countryside, the river _____

_____

_____ **3.** The frigid winter air _____

_____

_____ **4.** The dilapidated house at the end of the lane _____

_____

_____ **5.** Suddenly the players became _____

_____

_____ **6.** Our refrigerator _____

_____

_____ **7.** The ancient California redwoods _____

_____

_____ **8.** By evening, a gentle summer breeze _____

_____

_____ **9.** After working out in the sun too long without sunscreen, her skin_____

_____

 Ads often use figurative language. Gather some old newspapers, magazines, and catalogs. Then find at least five examples of figurative language.

Writing Wonderful Words

Two other kinds of figurative language are **alliteration** *and* **assonance**. *They can also make your stories and poems fun and interesting.* **Alliteration** *is the repetition of a consonant sound at the beginning of words.*

> **Benjamin Barker loves to bake**
> **Buns and biscuits and buttery cakes,**
> **Breads and brownies and blackberry pies,**
> **Apple brown betty and berry surprise!**

Assonance *is the repetition of the same vowel sounds either at the beginning of words or inside the words.*

> **Anna's nana asked for bananas and apples—just a few!**
> **And apricots and anchovies and abalone stew!**
> **Antipasto with avocados and ash bread! PHEW!**

Underline the letters used to make alliteration or assonance in each group of words. Choose one example of each and list words with the same repeated consonant or vowel sound. You can use a dictionary. Then use the words to write silly sentences or a poem on the lines.

Phyllis the famous photographer	abruptly announced	bellowing yellow yak
everyone excitedly exclaimed	perfect piece of pie	obstinate tot named Otto
impudent imp implored	creepy crawly critter	whittled and whistled
slowly slithering serpent	an uncouth youth	groggy grizzly growled

_____   _____

_____ _____   _____ _____

_____ _____   _____ _____

_____ _____   _____ _____

_____ _____   _____ _____

_____   _____

_____   _____

_____   _____

Write each letter of your name on a separate line along the left margin on another sheet of paper. Then write phrases using alliteration or assonance to describe yourself.